A Bad Influence

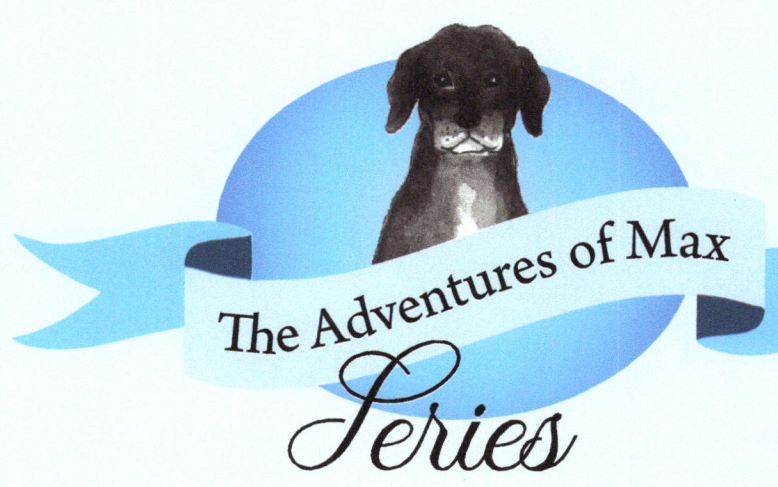

The Adventures of Max Series

Book Seven

Written by Warren Ravenscroft
Illustrations by Zoe Jones

The Adventures of Max: A Bad Influence
© Warren Ravenscroft 2021

Written by Warren Ravenscroft
Illustration by Zoe Jones of Zoe Jones Art

All rights reserved. No part of this publication may be reproduced, stored in a retrieval system, or transmitted in any form or by any means, electronic, mechanical, photocopying, recording or otherwise, without the prior written permission of the author.

ISBN: 978-0-6451837-8-8 Paperback

 A catalogue record for this book is available from the National Library of Australia

Scripture taken from the Spirit Filled Life Bible New King James Version®.
Copyright © 1991 by Thomas Nelson, Inc.
Used by permission. All rights reserved.

Published by Warren Ravenscroft
Website: www.wittonbooks.com

Illustrated by Zoe Jones
Zoe Jones Art and Design
Website: www.zoejonesart.com

The Fall.
Genesis 3: 1–24

Breakfast was over, and Max made his way to the front verandah where he knew George would soon join him to read the morning paper.

Max looked forward to this time; with all the chores completed, he could enjoy a time of rest.

As he slept peacefully, Max was suddenly woken from the catnap he was enjoying.

He could hear the phone ringing.

This didn't happen very often but, when it did, it was usually important.

Mary appeared at the door.

'George, Helen just rang. Her two dogs are sick and she would like you to go and have a look at them. The vet is away tending to other animals,' said Mary.

George stood and looked at Max who was now waiting expectantly to find out what would happen next.

'Come on, Max,' said George. 'Looks like we need to go for a drive.'

George reversed the ute out of the garage.

He opened the front door and Max jumped in, eager to take his seat.
This was where Max sat when travelling alone with George in the ute.

*Helen. Yes, she has my friends: Chubbs and Lady.
Oh, I do hope they are all right,* thought Max.

Max had only been to Helen's property once before.

He remembered that she had a big house with an abundance of green grass and a lake where native animals and birds came to drink. Some made their home there.

Helen grew vegetables and had many fruit trees of all different types.

This setting appealed to Max as it gave him feelings of peace and quiet with nothing to disturb him.

George pulled up to the gate of Helen's property.

He opened the gate and drove through—stopping to close the gate behind them—then continued down the winding track to the front of Helen's home.

As Max jumped from the ute, he was envious of the trees offering so much shade around the front lawn of her home.

Helen hurriedly made her way down the stairs and wasted no time telling George about her two dogs.

'Thank you for coming, George,' said Helen who was in somewhat of a panic. 'I have never seen my two dogs so sick. With the vet away, I did not know what to do, so I called Mary. I knew she would be able to help me. Come with me and you can see for yourself.'

George called Max to come, and the three of them made
their way to where the dogs lay on the back verandah.

Helen had made comfortable beds for her two precious ones to lie on.

As George looked at them, it was evident they were unwell.

Max walked slowly over to Chubbs and whispered,
'My owner George is here to help. What happened to you and Lady?'

Although Chubbs was not in a talkative mood, he said, 'We were running about in the field where the fruit trees are growing. We sometimes eat part of the fruit that has dropped on the ground, but we know what to eat and what will make us sick.'

'Lady went to the tree that's fenced off in the middle of the orchard. We have often been to this tree with Helen, but she never allows us to go inside the fence. She always makes sure the gate is closed, leaving us outside. We bark and whine, but she never lets us in.'

After a short pause to catch his breath, Chubbs continued. 'The gate was open this morning, so Lady decided to go inside. She returned and told me it was so cool and refreshing under the leaf-filled branches of this tree inside the enclosure, and I should follow her. She raced straight in, although I stopped at the gate.'

'Come on, she beckoned, so I did. Lady was right. It was the most wonderful place; exactly as she described it to me. It was nothing like the rest of the orchard. Lady noticed some fruit had fallen from the tree.

She sniffed it, then took a bite. She then woofed at me to have some as well.

I have to admit, it was really nice. I have never tasted anything like this before. We then decided to leave.' Chubbs paused again to regain some strength.

He was not feeling well.

'We were about halfway back to the house when Lady felt sick, having pains in most of her body. It wasn't long before I was experiencing the same symptoms. We barely made it back to our kennels when Helen saw us and phoned Mary to ask her advice. Thank you for coming.'

Max knew what he needed to do.

He barked and ran out the back door and down the steps.

'Where are you going, Max?' said George.

Max barked and ran across the lawn and into the paddock where the fruit trees were growing.

George quickly followed.

Max went straight to the tree in the enclosure. The gate was still open.

As George arrived, Max barked at the open gate.

George knew exactly what had happened.

'Good boy, Max,' said George. He closed and secured the gate and they quickly made their way back to where Helen was sitting with Chubbs and Lady.

George explained to Helen what he had found.

Helen gasped. 'Oh no! That's a very special tree, unlike the rest of the trees. I keep it separate for a reason: while it looks lovely in every way—the fruit looks enticing and smells good—it can make you very sick if it's not prepared and cooked properly.

I will ring the vet again and leave a message for him, as I know he has the correct medicine to cure my dogs,' said Helen.

When the vet received the message, he knew this was an emergency, and made his way immediately to the property. George and Max waited at the front gate. When the vet arrived, they led him to where Chubbs and Lady were laying.

After a quick examination of both dogs, the vet gave them both a needle to make them well again.

Helen thanked George, then knelt down and gave Max a big hug and said, 'Thank you.' Max just barked.

Together, George and Max left Helen with the vet and returned to the ute where Max sat in his seat, and they made their way home to Mary.

Have you ever seen or been to a place where it looked really great?

You just wanted to go and enjoy yourself, but your mum or dad said no?

There is always a reason why we are told no.

Although it may seem unfair at the time, we need to do what we are told.

By disobeying, we are doing wrong and this can sometimes lead to us being punished, even when we are sorry for what we did.

When you do wrong, and you ask Jesus to forgive you, He will—no questions asked—when He knows you are sincere.

Jesus wants to be your friend.

Why not ask Him to be your friend today?

Notes to parents and carers

Children love to revisit their favourite stories, and each rereading provides an opportunity to dig deeper into the text and reveal a fresh layer of meaning.

The Adventures of Max can be enjoyed in three ways:

- as simple children's narratives
- at a deeper level by making connections to our own lives and values
- in relation to the parables, Jesus told in the Bible.

Reading to young children (three to five years of age)

Initial readings should focus on the story and illustration. Encourage the children to comment on the pictures and make connections to their own world:

- What awakened Max from his sleep?
- How did Max react when George said they were going for a drive?
- What did Max remember about Helen's home as he was travelling with Max?
- What did Max do when Chubbs finished telling him what had happened that morning?
- What did Max do when arriving at the open gate of the fenced tree?
- What did George say to Max about how he acted and helped
- How do you think Max would have felt about being able to help his friends?

Subsequent reading can focus on making connections to the child's own life:

- What rules does your family have in place to keep you safe?
- Do you listen to your parents when they tell you not to touch something or go somewhere?
- What could you say to your friends when they ask you to do something you know is wrong?
- Will you remember the story of *A Bad Influence* next time you hear a friend needs help?

Reading to older children

In the Bible, Genesis 3: 1-24, tells us how disobedience and sin separated us from God. Read these verses to your child then:

- Discuss the similarities between the story of Adam and Eve, and the story of *A Bad Influence* (e.g. understanding what is said, stubborn, willfulness, disobedience, going your own way).
- What was the one instruction God gave to Adam and Eve?
- What was the consequence of their disobedience?
- What guidance does God provide for your safety and happiness today?
- What do you see as the main message in the two stories?
- How does this apply to your lives?

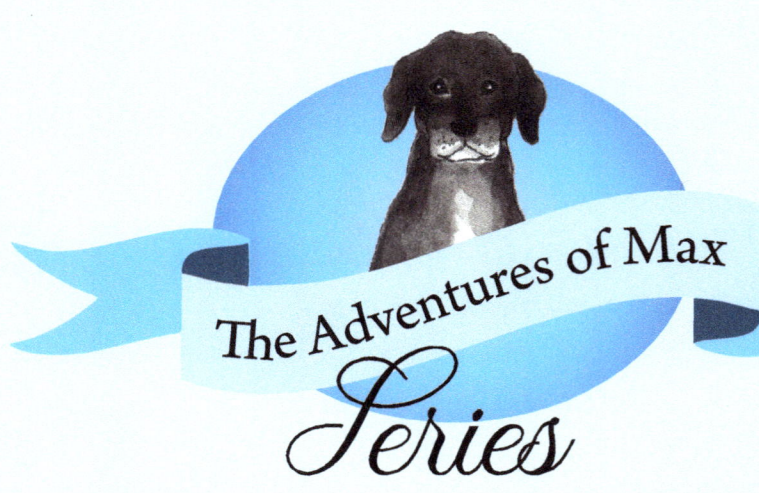

The Adventures of Max Series

Series titles available:

Book One	*The Defiant Mouse*
Book Two	*The Curious Chicken*
Book Three	*A Dog in Need*
Book Four	*An Old Friend Found*
Book Five	*The Rescue*
Book Six	*The Bush Fire*
Book Seven	*A Bad Influence*
Book Eight	*A Shining Light*
Book Nine	*Hidden Secrets*
Book Ten	*A Foiled Plot*
Book Eleven	*Running the Race*
Book Twelve	*An Unexpected Reward*
Book Thirteen	*Max Meets a Friend*
Book Fourteen	*Reflections*

Books available from *The Adventures of Max* Facebook page, and www.wittonbooks.com

Other books by the Author

Have you ever searched the four gospels to obtain the full account of Jesus life?

The Author, under their guidance of the Holy Spirit, took the words of the Apostle Paul to heart, when he wrote to Timothy and encouraged him to: "Study to show yourself approved unto God, a workman that needs not be ashamed, rightly dividing the word of truth".
2 Timothy 2:15.

The Life of Jesus
A Simple Narrative

In 'The Life of Jesus. A Simple Narrative', the author used language, similar to the New King James Version of the Bible to order and blend the four gospels into one complete story.

The Life of Christ
Simply Told

In the Second book, 'The Life of Christ Simply Told', the author used language, similar to the New International Version of the Bible to order and blend the four gospels into the complete story of Jesus life.

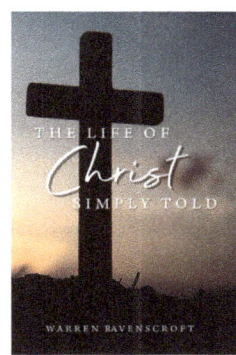

www.ingramcontent.com/pod-product-compliance
Lightning Source LLC
Chambersburg PA
CBHW061801290426
44109CB00030B/2915